TEN
COPYCATS
IN A BOAT
and Other Riddles

D1535300

TEN COPYCATS IN A BOAT

and Other Riddles

by ALVIN SCHWARTZ

Pictures by
MARC SIMONT

SCHOLASTIC BOOK SERVICES
NEW YORK · TORONTO · LONDON · AUCKLAND · SYDNEY · TOKYO

ISBN 0-590-32262-1

Text copyright © 1980 by Alvin Schwartz. Illustrations copyright © 1980 by Marc Simont. All rights reserved. This edition is published by Scholastic Book Services, a division of Scholastic Inc., 50 West 44 Street, New York, N.Y. 10036, by arrangement with Harper & Row Publishers, Inc.

12 11 10 9 8 7 6 5 4 3 2 1   9   1 2 3 4 5 6/8

Ten copycats were sitting in a boat,

and one jumped out.

How many were left?

None. They all were copycats.

What does a cat have

that no other animal has?

Kittens.

If you put four ducks in a box,
what would you have?

A box of quackers.

What has two heads, four eyes,

six legs, and a tail?

A horse and a rider.

What is

over your head

and under your hat?

13

Your hair.

A baseball team scored six runs

in one inning,

but not one man reached home.

Why not?

It was a girls' team.

If you threw a white stone

into the Red Sea,

what would it become?

17

Wet.

What gets wetter and wetter

the more it dries?

19

A towel.

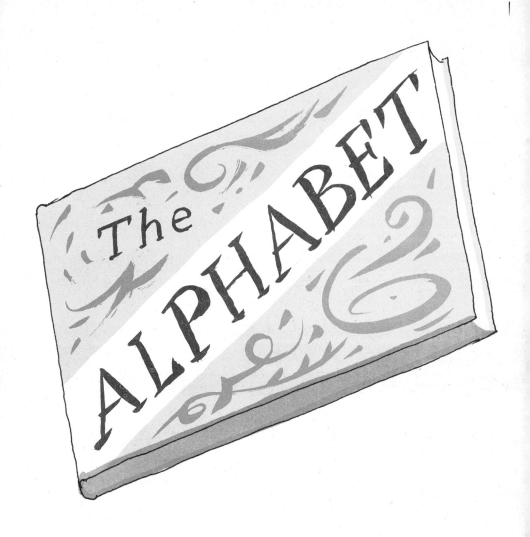

How many letters are there in the alphabet?

Eleven.

The ALPHABET

"Never use the letter D."

"Why not?"

"It makes Ma mad."

What word does everybody say wrong?

Wrong!

What is the longest word

in the world?

SMILES.

There is a mile

between the first letter

and the last letter.

What is as big as an elephant,

but weighs nothing at all?

The shadow of an elephant.

Why do dragons sleep all day?

They like to hunt knights.

What always sleeps

with its shoes on?

A horse.

"What is yellow and brown

and has a hundred legs?"

"I don't know."

"I don't know either, but...

35

it is crawling up your neck!"

Why shouldn't you tell secrets

on a farm?

The corn has ears.

The potatoes have eyes.

And the beanstalk.

What did the pig say

when the farmer grabbed its tail?

That is the end of me!

An eagle flew through the sky,

and a dog sat on its tail.

How could that be?

What is the best way

to catch a squirrel?

Climb into a tree

and act like a nut.

What is this a picture of?

Snow White in a snowstorm.

S	M	T	W	T	F	S
			1	2	3	4
5	6	7	8	9	10	11
12	13	14	15	16	17	18
19	20	21	22	23	24	25
26	27	28	29	30		

Where does Friday

come before Thursday?

In a dictionary.

When is a car not a car?

49

When it turns into

a parking lot.

How many sides

has a glass of lemonade?

Two—the inside and the outside.

What is the difference

between a jeweler

and a jailer?

53

A jeweler sells watches.

A jailer watches cells.

What invention

lets you look

right through a wall?

A window.

A boy fell off

a hundred-foot ladder.

But he did not get hurt.

Why didn't he?

He fell off the bottom step.

A girl dreamed

a lion was chasing her.

He was getting closer and closer.

Then she came to a tall tree.

And to escape

she climbed all the way

to the top.

But at the top

she found a giant snake.

So there she was

with a snake in the tree

and a lion on the ground.

How did she get away?

She woke up.

There are millions of riddles to tell.
Some are puzzles that make you think
good and hard. Others are jokes and tricks
that make you laugh good and hard.

They are found everywhere. Yet each was
created by an unknown person.

Many of these riddles are very old. The
riddle about a "monster" with two heads, on
page 11, is an example. It was used by some
children in England over three hundred
years ago.

Since then this riddle has traveled to
many places, including the place where
you live.